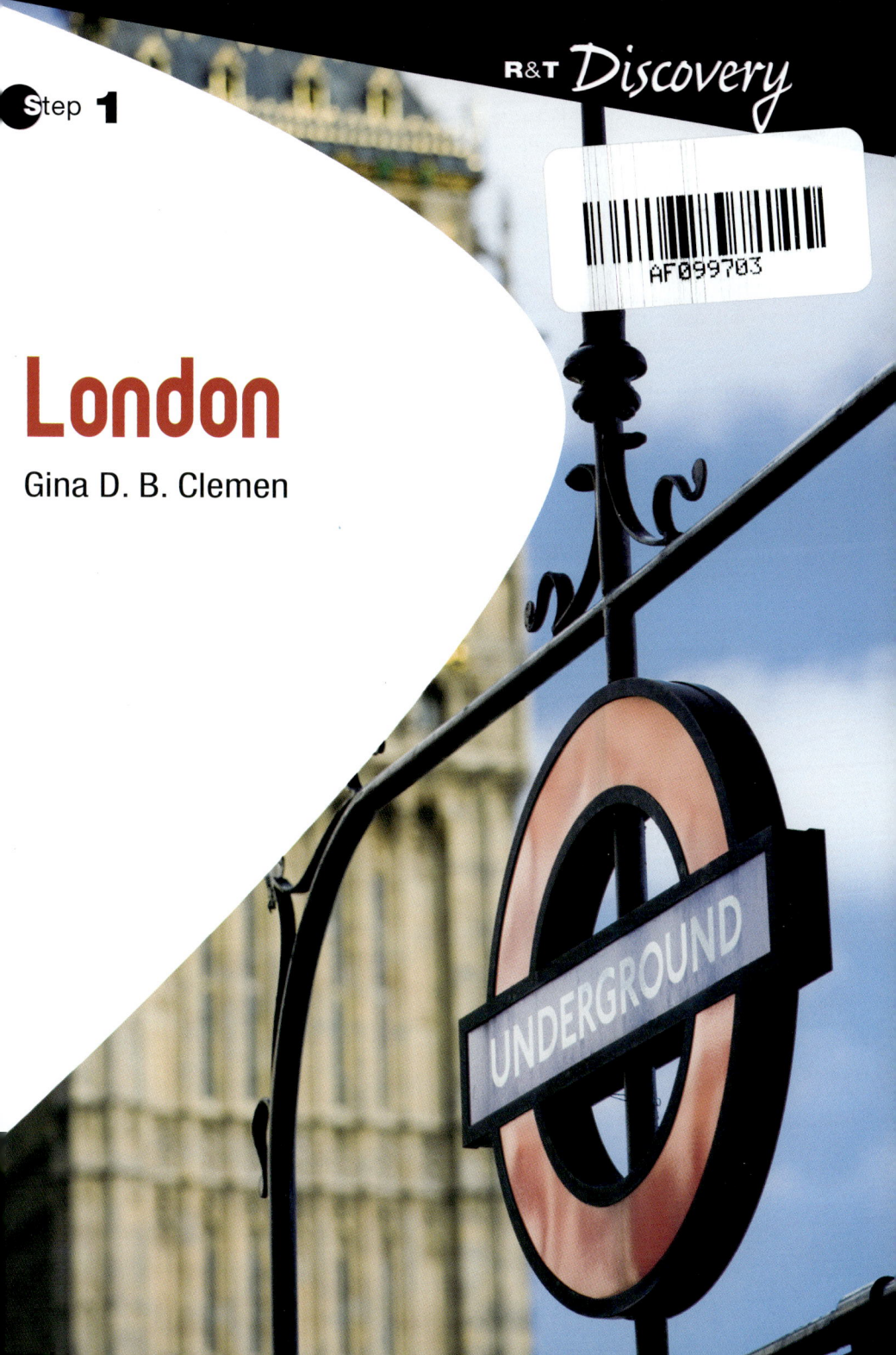

Step 1

R&T *Discovery*

London

Gina D. B. Clemen

Editor: Daniela Penzavalle
Design and art direction: Nadia Maestri
Computer graphics: Tiziana Pesce
Picture research: Laura Lagomarsino

© 2010   Black Cat

First edition: January 2010

DEALINK, DEAFLIX are trademarks licensed by De Agostini SpA

Picture credits
Getty images: front cover; Cideb archive; © MAPS.com/Corbis: 5 top; Michael Blann/ Getty Images: 5 bottom; Dorling Kindersley/Getty Images: 6, 87; © DBURKE /Alamy: 8; © The Trustees of the British Museum : 9 top; © World History Archive /Alamy: 9 centre; De Agostini Picture Library: 9 bottom, 13, 18, 19, 22, 31, 32, 48, 49, 51, 52, 53, 67 bottom, 71, 76; The Bridgeman Art Library/Getty images: 11, 12, 27, 28, 37, 38, 39, 40; SONY PICTURES/Album/Contrasto: 25; Erich Lessing Archive/Contrasto: 29; Hulton Archive/Getty Images: 42, 43, 44-45, 50; EIGHTFISH/Getty Images: 56; Rex Butcher/ Getty Images: 66; tips images: 62-63, 67 top, 72 bottom; Gary Yeowell/Getty images: 68; Douglas Pearson / Getty Images: 69; Lonely Planet Images/Getty Images: 72 top; Rex Butcher/Getty Images: 80; © Catherine Karnow/Corbis: 87 bottom.

All rights reserved. No part of this book may be reproduced, stored in a retrieval system, or transmitted, in any form or by any means, electronic, mechanical, photocopying, recording or otherwise, without the written permission of the publisher.

We would be happy to receive your comments and suggestions, and give you any other information concerning our material.
info@blackcat-cideb.com
blackcat-cideb.com

The Publisher is certified by
CISQCERT
in compliance with the UNI EN ISO 9001:2000 standards for the activities of 'Design, production, distribution and sale of publishing products.'
(certificate no. 04.953)

Printed in Italy by Italgrafica, Novara

Contents

INTRODUCTION		4
CHAPTER **ONE**	**The Beginnings**	7
CHAPTER **TWO**	**Elizabethan London**	18
CHAPTER **THREE**	**The Great Fire and the Rebuilding of London**	27
CHAPTER **FOUR**	**Dickens's London and the Early 20th Century**	37
CHAPTER **FIVE**	**Westminster Today**	55
CHAPTER **SIX**	**The West End**	65
CHAPTER **SEVEN**	**The City and Beyond**	83
DOSSIERS	London and Its Writers	48
	London's Parks and Museums	76

INTERNET PROJECTS   16, 26, 35, 47, 54, 75, 81, 89, 93

ACTIVITIES   14, 23, 33, 44, 61, 73, 90

AFTER READING   94

KET Cambridge KET-style activities   5, 14, 23, 24, 36, 44, 46, 61, 64, 74, 82, 90, 92

T: GRADES 3/4   Trinity-style activities   24, 62

The text is recorded in full.

 These symbols indicate the beginning and end of the passages linked to the listening activities.

Introduction

London is the capital of the United Kingdom and has a population of about 7,500,000. In the 19th century it was the biggest and most important city in the world, the centre of the great British Empire.

Today, London is not the biggest city in the world but it is still one of the most important business, financial, educational and cultural centres. It is an international city with people from all over the world who live and work there: more than 300 languages are spoken in London. After World War II (1939-45) two large groups of immigrants [1] settled in London: one group of people came from different parts of India, and the other group came from the Caribbean and African countries. There are, however, now as always, immigrants from all over the world.

London covers a very big area: about 1,610 sq km (620 sq miles). This area is divided into thirty-two boroughs [2] and the City of London which is a separate political unit. Most of Central London is located north of the River Thames and includes the City of London, Westminster and the West End. London has many suburbs. [3]

The book you are going to read will introduce you to one of the world's most exciting and interesting cities, where there is always a lot to see and do.

1. **immigrants** : people who leave their native country and go to live and work in another country.
2. **boroughs** : parts of a big city which have their own local governments.
3. **suburbs** : the parts of a city outside the centre where people live.

KET ① Complete these notes about London.

LONDON
Capital of: (1) ....
Population: (2) ....
Area: (3) ....
Number of boroughs: (4) ....
Main groups of immigrants from:
(5) ....
....
....

1 ACTIVITIES

Before you read

1 Vocabulary

Match the words (1-8) with the parts of the town (A-H). Use a dictionary to help you.

1 wooden bridge
2 warehouse
3 temple
4 amphitheatre
5 fort
6 forum
7 basilica
8 city gate

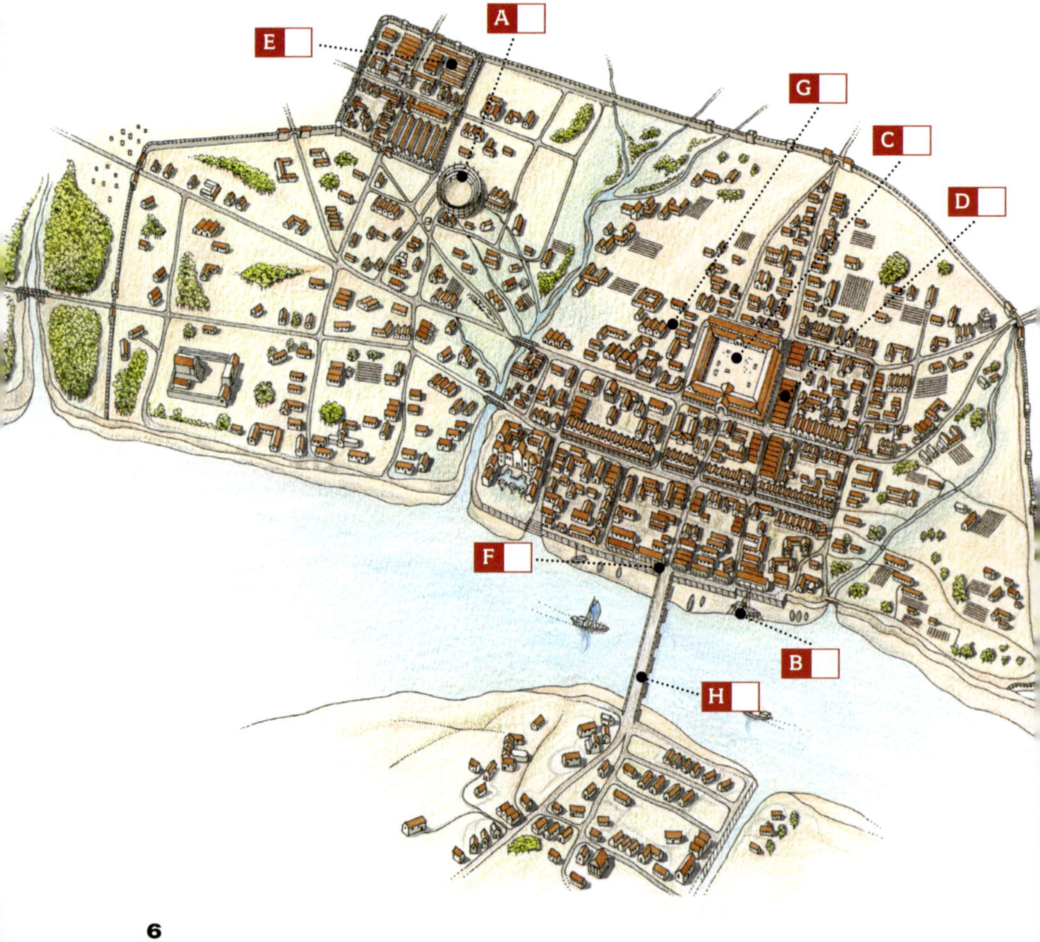

CHAPTER **ONE**

The Beginnings

*The Romans gave Britain a written
language, written numbers,
a ten-month calendar
and excellent roads.*

Roman Londinium

In 43 CE the Roman Emperor Claudius sent an army of 40,000 soldiers to invade Britain. Shortly after, the Romans founded the town of Londinium on the north side of the River Thames, where the City of London stands today.

The Roman soldiers built a wooden bridge across the River Thames just east of the present London Bridge. Along the river there was a wharf for ships and warehouses for goods. The Roman historian Tacitus wrote that Londinium became a busy centre for trade. [1]

Early Londinium was a small town, about the size of one of modern London's big parks. It looked like most other Roman towns, with a rectangular plan and two main streets that

---

1. **trade** : when people buy and sell goods.

London

crossed each other, and at the centre there was the forum. This was a square with a market, shops and a big town hall called the basilica.

Around the year 60 CE Londinium was attacked and destroyed by the Iceni people led by Queen Boudicca, who was against the Romans. However, the town was soon rebuilt and it became an important military and centre for trade. By 100 CE Londinium had a population of about 65,000 and became the capital of the Roman province of Britannia. In Londinium the Romans built beautiful homes, important public buildings, a large basilica, a governor's palace, temples, bathhouses, an amphitheatre and a large fort for the soldiers.

Six important Roman roads started in or passed through Londinium; one of the most famous was Watling Street. It was an old road that went from Wales to Dover and it was improved by the Romans. People still use it today.

Walking tour group visiting the London Wall in Barbican, London; remnants of the old Roman wall that defended Londinium.

The Beginnings

Between the years 190 and 225 CE a wall of about three kilometres was built around the northern part of Londinium to protect [2] it. In the later part of the third century Londinium was attacked by Saxon pirates, so another wall was built along the River Thames. This wall lasted about 1,600 years and six of the seven traditional city gates were of Roman origin — Aldersgate, Aldgate, Bishopgate, Cripplegate, Ludgate and Newgate — except Moorgate, which was of Medieval origin. Today you can see parts of the old Roman walls at the Museum of London, along with beautiful Roman mosaic floors and other objects.

During the third century there were problems in the Roman Empire, but Londinium continued to grow bigger and richer. At the beginning of the fifth century Rome was attacked by people from northern Europe. In 407 CE Emperor Constantine III called the Roman army back to Rome to

Roman mosaic found under the Bank of England in the City of London.

Marble head of the god Serapis found in London.

2. **protect** : to keep safe.

London

protect the empire. The last Roman soldiers left Britain in 410 CE. This was the end of Roman rule in Britain and, of course, in Londinium. By the end of the fifth century most of Londinium was in ruins [3] and was attacked by invaders.

Medieval London

Little is known about London after the Romans left, but historians tell us that the city was mostly in ruins. By the late 600s a Saxon village and trading centre was founded about one mile to the west of Londinium, near what is now the Covent Garden area of London. This village grew until the Vikings, people from Scandinavia, attacked Britain in the ninth century. Then the village moved to Roman Londinium, where the old city walls protected it. Viking attacks continued in south-east England until 886, when King Alfred the Great made peace with the Viking leader. King Alfred rebuilt the Roman walls around the village and it slowly became an important town again.

    The Saxon Edward, called 'the Confessor' because he was very religious, was king between 1042 and 1066. He moved his palace two miles west of the town to Westminster because he was building a great church there, Westminster Abbey. Westminster, with its beautiful palace and abbey, became the centre of government and religion. The king and the nobles lived there. The City of London became the centre of business and trade with its narrow [4] streets and small shops, and the merchants [5] lived here. This difference between Westminster and The City of London lasted through the centuries and is still true today.

3. **in ruins** : with many buildings broken and falling down.
4. **narrow** : thin, not wide, small.
5. **merchants** : people who buy and sell goods.

The Beginnings

The Normans — the word comes from 'Northmen' — were Vikings who went to live in northwest France in the early 900s. They gave their name to that area of France: Normandy. When Edward the Confessor died, two men wanted to be king of England: William, Duke of Normandy and Harold Godwinsson. When Harold became king, William was very angry because Edward the Confessor promised him the throne. 6 William decided to invade England in 1066: this was the beginning of the Medieval period. After winning the Battle of Hastings in 1066, William the Conqueror became the first Norman King of England. He built the White Tower, which is now part of the Tower of London, and gave the City the right to its own government.

Tower of London seen from the River Thames, from *A Book of the Prospects of the Remarkable Places in and about the City of London* (1700).

6. **promised him the throne** : said he could be the king of England.

London

The Normans built old St Paul's Cathedral between 1087 and 1314, where the new St Paul's Cathedral is today. In 1209 London Bridge was rebuilt in stone; it was the only bridge across the River Thames until 1750. There were many houses and shops on it.

Medieval London grew quickly with its small shops and houses along narrow streets. Rich merchants and artisans [7] in the City started guilds. [8] The centre of government in the City was — and still is — the Guildhall, which was built in the 15th century. Many

Old London Bridge, detail from *Vischer's London* (17th century).

7. **artisans** : people who make things with their hands and sell them.
8. **guilds** : organizations of people who do the same job or activity.

The Beginnings

The Guildhall, London.

of the streets in the City were named after the jobs of artisans or merchants. For example, Bread Street had bakeries and Milk Street is where cows were kept. Today many streets in the City still have the medieval names of jobs.

In the 1400s London became the centre of international wool trade, and the first banks were started by Italian bankers. The banking centre was — and still is — Lombard Street (named after Lombardy, an area of north Italy). Its port on the River Thames was a busy place, with a lot of ships and warehouses, because London traded goods with all of Europe. In the early 1500s its population grew to about 40,000.

1 ACTIVITIES

The text and **beyond**

KET 1 Comprehension check

Are these sentences 'Right' (A) or 'Wrong' (B)? If there is not enough information to answer 'Right' or 'Wrong', choose 'Doesn't say' (C). There is an example at the beginning (0).

		A	B	C
0	The Roman army invaded Britain in 43 CE.	✓		
1	Tacitus was a Roman soldier.			
2	Londinium became one of London's big parks.			
3	Londinium was an important town and became the capital of Britannia in the year 100 CE.			
4	Watling Street was two hundred kilometers long.			
5	The Roman army had to go back to Rome because there were problems in the empire.			
6	In the ninth century the Vikings built walls around Londinium to protect it.			
7	Westminster Abbey was built by King Edward the Confessor.			
8	The king and the nobles lived in the City and the merchants lived in Westminster.			
9	The Normans won the Battle of Hastings in 1066.			
10	It took thirty-five years to rebuild London Bridge in stone.			
11	In the fifteenth century London was a poor city.			
12	Italian bankers started the first London banks.			

ACTIVITIES 1

2 Who was it?

Match the descriptions (1-12) with the names (A-J). You can use a name more than once.

1. ☐ He built the White Tower.
2. ☐ He called the Roman army back to Rome.
3. ☐ He made peace with the Viking leader.
4. ☐ They built a long wall along the northern part of Londinium.
5. ☐ He fought in the Battle of Hastings.
6. ☐ He sent a big army to invade Britain.
7. ☐ They built old St Paul's Cathedral.
8. ☐ They invaded Britain in the ninth century.
9. ☐ They set up the first banks in London.
10. ☐ He was a Roman historian who wrote about Londinium.
11. ☐ They built a wooden bridge across the River Thames.
12. ☐ He built Westminster Abbey.

A King Alfred the Great
B The Vikings
C Emperor Claudius
D Tacitus
E King Edward the Confessor
F The Romans
G Emperor Constantine III
H Italian bankers
I The Normans
J William the Conqueror

Choose three names and write a sentence about each one similar to 1-12 above. Then read your sentences to the class. Can the class guess who they are?

15

1 ACTIVITIES

INTERNET PROJECT

Let's visit Roman Londinium!

Connect to the internet and go to www.blackcat-cideb.com. Insert the title of the book into our search engine. Open the page for *London*. Click on the Internet project link. Go down the page until you find the title of this book and click on the relevant link for this project.

The Romans left Britain a written language, written numbers, a ten-month calendar and many excellent roads. Let's see how they lived in Britannia.

Divide the class into six groups. Each group will chose one of the icons at the top of the site 'Digging up the Romans': People, Town Life, Invasion and Settlement, Army, Beliefs and Crafts, Roads and Trade. Prepare a brief report on the topic and tell the class about it.

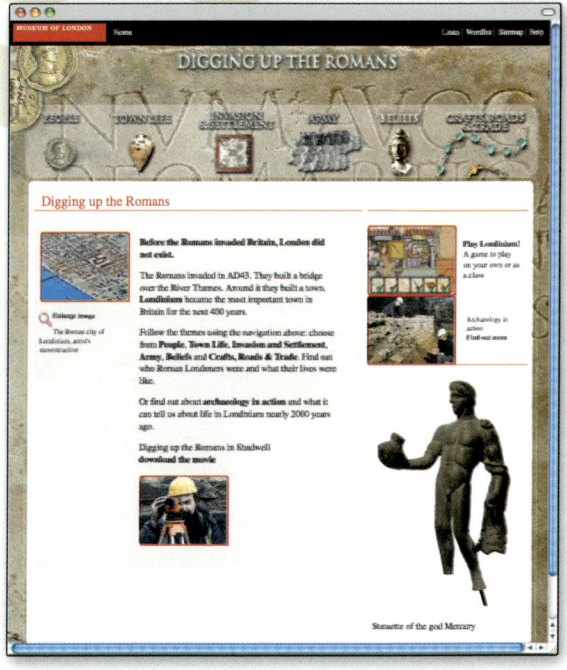

ACTIVITIES 2

Before you read

1 Vocabulary
Match the words (1-3) with the parts of the theatre.

1 galleries   2 yard or pit   3 stage

2 Reading pictures
Look at the picture of Queen Elizabeth on p. 19 and answer these questions.

1   What is the queen's dress like?
2   Where is the queen's right hand? Why do you think it is there?
3   Describe the two paintings in the background. What do you think they refer to?

17

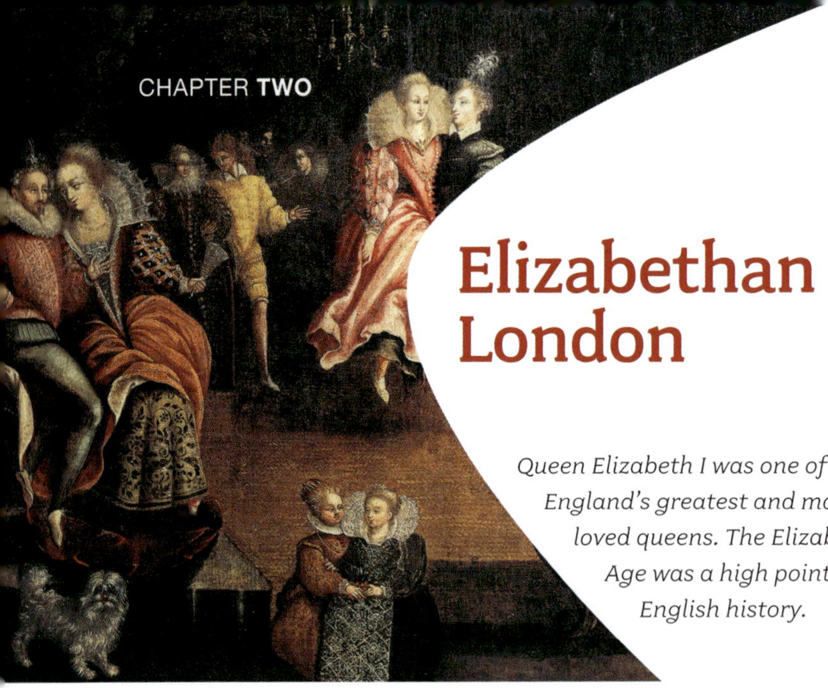

CHAPTER **TWO**

Elizabethan London

Queen Elizabeth I was one of England's greatest and most loved queens. The Elizabethan Age was a high point in English history.

The period when Elizabeth I was queen — 1558 to 1603 — is known as the Elizabethan Age, and it was one of the most interesting and exciting periods in English history. It was a time of exploration, discovery and growth of the arts and the theatre. Elizabeth's reign [1] was the high point of the English Renaissance [2] (early 16th to early 17th century).

What was Elizabethan London like?

About 200,000 people lived in London at that time and its streets were narrow, crowded, [3] dirty and noisy. There was a lot of crime because there were no policemen.

1. **reign** : the period of time a king or queen is in power.
2. **Renaissance** : the period in Europe between the 14th and 16th centuries when there was a great interest in the arts and sciences. It arrived later in England.
3. **crowded** : full of people.

Elizabethan London

The Armada Portrait of Queen Elizabeth (about 1588) by George Gower.

A new kind of entertainment in Elizabethan London was the open-air theatre, where actors performed plays. Theatres were not allowed in London because the local government thought plays were not good entertainment for the people, so they were built outside the city. Some theatres were built north of London and others south of the River Thames in the borough of Southwark. In Elizabethan London, Southwark was the entertainment centre, with theatres and taverns. [4]

In 1576 the first open-air theatre was built by James Burbage in Shoreditch, which was north of London. It was called The

---

4. **taverns** : places where people went to eat, drink and have fun.

The Shakespeare Globe Theatre today.

Theatre. The richer members of the audience [5] sat in the galleries and the poorer members stood in the yard. Soon other theatres like The Rose, The Swan and The Globe were built. Both rich and poor people loved going to the theatre and tickets cost very little. At that time all the women's parts were played by young men because women were not allowed to work in the theatre.

Many new acting companies were formed and rich men — called patrons — helped them with money. One of the most famous acting companies was called the Lord Chamberlain's Men, where William Shakespeare worked as an actor and playwright. [6] His plays were very popular in London and even Queen Elizabeth I enjoyed watching them.

In 1599 Shakespeare and the Lord Chamberlain's Men built their own theatre in Southwark; it was called The Globe and it

5. **audience** : people who go to see a performance.
6. **playwright** : a person who writes plays.

was very successful. A fire destroyed it in 1613, but today you can watch one of Shakespeare's play at the new Globe Theatre, which was rebuilt in Southwark in 1996.

Queen Elizabeth liked music and dancing, and these two kinds of entertainment became popular when she was queen. She was a great patron of the arts and many musicians, playwrights, poets and artists worked for her. Two of England's finest musicians, Thomas Tallis and William Byrd, worked for the Queen. Elizabeth loved the theatre and had her own company of actors called the Queen's Men.

The artist Nicholas Hilliard painted miniature portraits [7] of Elizabeth and several people of her court. Thanks to him, we are able to see what people in Elizabethan London looked like.

Exploration and discovery

The Elizabethan Age was a time of exploration and discovery. Sir Francis Drake was a great explorer and sea captain. In 1577 he was the first Englishman to sail around the world. At that time Spain was a strong, rich country with colonies [8] in the New World, and an enemy of England. Queen Elizabeth asked Drake to attack Spanish ships and take their gold and treasure, which he brought to the Queen. In 1585 Sir Walter Raleigh started the first English colony in the New World. It was called Roanoke Island, on the Atlantic Coast of America. The colony

7. **miniature portraits**: very small paintings of people.
8. **colonies**: territories governed by another country.

London

failed but it was the beginning of English colonization in the New World. He also founded Virginia, which he named in honour of Queen Elizabeth.

In 1588 the English navy won a big sea battle against the Spanish Armada. The Armada was a big group of about 130 ships and 28,000 men that attacked England. This made England the strongest country in Europe at that time.

Many other things were happening in Elizabethan London. In 1565 the Royal Exchange was built by Sir Thomas Gresham and opened by the Queen. It was a kind of Elizabethan shopping mall, with many fine shops. In 1600 the English East India Company was founded and merchants began trading with India. The East India Company grew and was very important in the colonization of India.

Launch of Fireships against the Armada (16th century), Nederlandish School.

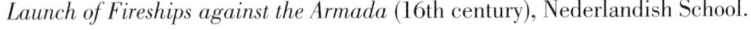

ACTIVITIES 2

The text and **beyond**

1 Comprehension check

Choose the correct answer — A, B or C.

1 Elizabeth became queen in
  - A ☐ 1603
  - B ☐ 1558
  - C ☐ 1600

2 Theatres were built outside London
  - A ☐ because there was no space in the city.
  - B ☐ because Queen Elizabeth did not like the theatre.
  - C ☐ because they were not allowed in the city.

3 In 1576 James Burbage built the first open-air theatre
  - A ☐ called The Globe.
  - B ☐ north of London.
  - C ☐ where tickets were free.

4 William Shakespeare was an actor and playwright
  - A ☐ and worked with the Lord Chamberlain's Men.
  - B ☐ who wrote musical plays.
  - C ☐ and worked with the Queen's Men.

5 Roanoke Island was
  - A ☐ Sir Walter Raleigh's home town.
  - B ☐ a colony set up by Sir Francis Drake.
  - C ☐ England's first colony in the New World.

6 The English East India Company
  - A ☐ wanted to trade with India.
  - B ☐ set up colonies in the New World.
  - C ☐ belonged to Sir Francis Drake.

2 ACTIVITIES

KET 2 Vocabulary

A Read the definitions. What is the word for each one? The first letter is already there. There is one space for each other letter in the word. There is an example at the beginning (0).

0 A person who acts in plays.   a c t o r
1 A territory governed by another nation.   c _ _ _ _ _
2 The period of time when a king or queen
   is in power.   r _ _ _ _
3 A place where people went to eat, drink
   and have fun.   t _ _ _ _ _
4 A person who writes plays.   p _ _ _ _ _ _ _ _ _
5 People who play music.   m _ _ _ _ _ _ _ _

B In your notebooks write one sentence for each of the words.

T: GRADE 3

3 Speaking: jobs

William Shakespeare was a playwright and an actor. Sir Francis Drake was a navigator and an explorer. Talk about jobs with your partner. Use these questions to help you.

1 What job do you want to do and why?
2 Do you know someone who does this job?
3 What do you like about this job?
4 What school subjects do you need to study to do this job?
5 At what age can you start working in your country?

ACTIVITIES 2

4 Fill in the gaps

Read the text about William Shakespeare and fill in the gaps with the correct verb in the past tense. You can use a verb more than once. There is an example at the beginning (0).

> go be die marry have write change
> become leave receive join

William Shakespeare is probably the most famous playwright in the world, but we don't know a lot about his life. He (0) **was** born in 1564, probably on 23 April in Stratford-on-Avon, England. His father (1).......... a merchant and young Shakespeare (2).......... to grammar school in Stratford. Here he (3).......... a good education.

At the age of eighteen Shakespeare (4).......... Anne Hathaway, who was eight years older than him. They (5).......... three children, two girls and a boy. In the 1580s Shakespeare (6).......... his family and (7).......... to London to work as an actor. He (8).......... a theatrical company called the Lord Chamberlain's Men where he (9).......... a fine actor and a famous playwright. In 1603 the company's name (10).......... to the King's Men when James I (11).......... king.

Most of his plays (12).......... written between the 1590s and 1612. He (13).......... 38 great plays, including comedies, tragedies and histories. In 1612 he moved back to Stratford and (14).......... there on 23 April 1616. Today after four hundred years people still love going to the theatre and watching his great plays. Some of his most-loved plays are: *Romeo and Juliet, Hamlet, Macbeth, A Midsummer Night's Dream* and *The Merchant of Venice*.

Scene from the film
The Merchant of Venice (2004)
directed by Michael Radford.

2 ACTIVITIES

INTERNET PROJECT

Let's find out more about the Globe Theatre!
Look under Background. Divide the class into four groups and each group can prepare a brief report on:
- Shakespeare in London
- The First Globe
- Rebuilding the Globe
- Sam Wanamaker

Present your report to the class and put your reports on the class bulletin board. Then click on Virtual Tour and take a look at the stage, the yard and the galleries. Compare the old Globe Theatre to modern theatres. Which things are similar and which are different? Which do you like best and why?

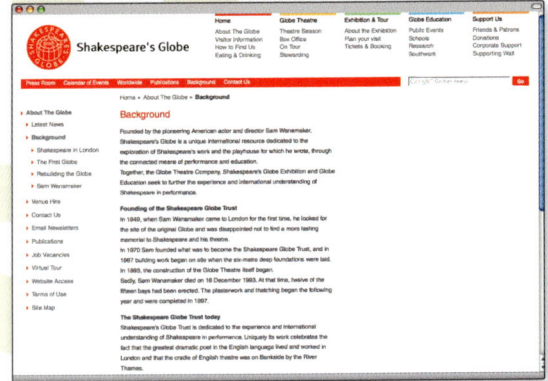

Before you read

① Vocabulary

Match the words (1-4) with their meanings (A-D). Use a dictionary to help you.

1. ☐ disaster
2. ☐ appearance
3. ☐ professionals
4. ☐ architect

A Doctors, lawyers, government officials and people with similar jobs.
B A person who designs buildings.
C An unexpected event that causes death, destruction and suffering.
D The way a place looks.

CHAPTER **THREE**

The Great Fire and the Rebuilding of London

Queen Elizabeth died without an heir,[1] so King James I became King of England in 1603. At the time he was King of Scotland too, so Scotland and England were united.

Inigo Jones (1573-1652)

When James I was king, London's appearance changed a lot because of the great architect Inigo Jones. He was one of the first Englishmen who studied architecture in Italy and brought Renaissance architecture to England. Jones's best-known buildings are the Queen's house at Greenwich and the Banqueting House at Whitehall. In 1631 Jones designed one of London's first squares, Covent Garden Piazza. Because he studied architecture in Italy, he called this square a 'piazza', the Italian word for a square. A lot of building went on in London during this time and you can still see Jones's beautiful works today.

1. **heir** : the son or daughter of a king or queen who becomes king or queen after the death of the parent.

27

View of Covent Garden (18th century) by Joseph van Aken.

The Great Plague

During the reign of King Charles II two terrible disasters hit London: the Great Plague of 1665 and the Great Fire of 1666. Today we know a lot about these disasters thanks to Samuel Pepys's diary. Pepys began keeping a diary in 1660 and it gives us a good picture of London life at that time. His diary describes the Great Plague and the Great Fire.

The plague began in the spring of 1665. It was another attack of the terrible bubonic plague which killed thousands of people during the Middle Ages all over Europe. The plague was spread [2] by fleas carried by rats through London's crowded, dirty streets. Everyone was afraid because there was no way to get better and people died everywhere. Richer people left London and went to live in the country, but most people had to stay in the city. This terrible plague went on for many months and about 100,000 people died, about a fifth of London's population.

2. **spread** : carried everywhere.

The Great Fire and the Rebuilding of London

The Great Fire

The second disaster was the Great Fire, which started on 2 September 1666 in a bakery in Pudding Lane. People tried to stop the terrible fire but they couldn't. Samuel Pepys and a friend watched the fire from the top of a church and they could see old St Paul's Cathedral burning. Pepys wrote that he saw 'poor people… running into boats, sick people carried away in bed'. People ran from their homes carrying few things with them. The fire spread everywhere for four days and quickly destroyed the many wooden buildings.

The Great Fire killed only nine people but destroyed most of London: about 13,200 buildings, 87 churches, 52 guildhalls and old St Paul's Cathedral. Luckily the Tower of London, Westminster Abbey and Westminster Hall, Temple Church and the Guildhall were not destroyed by the fire; we can still see them today.

The Great Fire of London (1666), Dutch School.

London

Christopher Wren (1632-1723)

King Charles II asked the great English architect Sir Christopher Wren to rebuild London. Wren prepared many plans to change and improve most of London's medieval streets, but only some of his plans were accepted. Many of London's narrow streets became wider, [3] and houses and buildings were built with bricks [4] instead of wood. Bricks were much safer in case of fire.

Wren directed all the work on royal palaces and government buildings in London and in most of Britain. In 1675 he started designing the new Saint Paul's Cathedral, which became a symbol of London with its great dome. It took Wren thirty-five years to complete it and it became his best-known work. He also designed and rebuilt fifty-three other beautiful churches in London. To remember the Great Fire, Wren designed and built The Monument, which is a 62-metre-high stone column with a golden ball at the top. It stands near Pudding Lane in the City, where the fire started. Visitors can go to the top, from where there are great views of London.

Saint Paul's Cathedral.

3. **wider** : something that measures a greater distance from one side to the other.

4. **bricks** :

The Great Fire and the Rebuilding of London

During the early years of the 18th century, the first newspapers were printed on Fleet Street.

The street was named after the River Fleet that runs under London's street near the River Thames.

A lot of building was going on at this time in London and the city grew. New areas like Mayfair were built for the rich in the West End.

Mayfair was named after the yearly May Fair that took place in the area. The fair was very big and lasted fifteen days. The rich families that built their beautiful homes in Mayfair did not like the noise and crowds of the yearly fair, so it was moved to another part of London.

Since there was a lot of crime in 18th-century London, the Bow Street Runners were set up in 1749 and they became the first professional police force. At first there were only eight policemen, but the number grew quickly.

Coffee houses, where men went to drink coffee, read the newspaper and meet with friends, became very popular in London.

Interior of a London Coffee House (18th century), English School.

London

The first coffeehouse was opened in London in 1652, in St Michael's Alley in the City.

By 1675 there were more than 3,000 coffeehouses in England. At first women were not allowed, but as time passed they started enjoying coffee in the many coffeehouses.

During the 18th and 19th centuries men began discussing important business in the coffeehouses.

View of the Grand Walk at the entrance of Vauxhall Pleasure Gardens (18th century).

A new kind of entertainment called 'the pleasure garden' became popular too. These beautiful pleasure gardens were like outdoor amusement parks [5] today, with musical concerts, fireworks [6] and other entertainment. Vauxhall Gardens and Ranelagh Gardens, in the Chelsea area, were the most famous.

5. amusement parks :  6. fireworks :

ACTIVITIES 3

The text and **beyond**

1 Comprehension check

Complete the sentences 1-9. Choose from the endings A-J. There is one extra sentence.

1. ☐ Inigo Jones was an important architect
2. ☐ The plague and the Great Fire took place
3. ☐ Samuel Pepys kept a diary about
4. ☐ The plague of 1665
5. ☐ The Great Fire of London
6. ☐ Most of London was destroyed
7. ☐ Much of London was rebuilt
8. ☐ The Monument in the City
9. ☐ Coffee houses became

A started in Pudding Lane in the City.
B remembers the Great Fire of 1666.
C who brought Renaissance architecture to England.
D during the first days of September 1666.
E by Christopher Wren.
F because Queen Elizabeth I died without an heir.
G during the reign of King Charles II.
H the plague and the Great Fire.
I popular meeting places for men.
J killed about 100,000 people.

3 ACTIVITIES

Many of London's narrow streets became wider.

Wider is the comparative form of **wide**.

To make the comparative of one-syllable adjectives we add **-er**.

old → old**er**   dark → dark**er**

When the adjective ends in consonant-vowel-consonant, we double the final consonant.

big → bi**gg**er   hot → ho**tt**er

For adjectives of two syllables ending in **-y**, we change the **-y** to **-i** and add **-er**.

easy → eas**ier**   happy → happ**ier**

For adjectives with two syllables or more we put **more** in front of the adjective.

difficult → **more** difficult   interesting → **more** interesting

Remember that **good** and **bad** have irregular comparatives.

good → **better**   bad → **worse**

2 Comparatives

Write the comparative form of the adjectives below.

1 beautiful ....   5 wide   ....
2 strong   ....   6 safe   ....
3 tall   ....   7 dirty   ....
4 long   ....   8 narrow ....

Complete the sentences with some of the comparatives above.

1 Covent Garden Piazza was .... than the dark, narrow streets.
2 Bricks were .... than wood in case of fire.
3 The dome of Saint Paul's Cathedral was .... than most buildings near it.
4 Sir Christopher Wren designed .... streets.
5 The plague lasted .... than the Great Fire.

ACTIVITIES 3

3 Vocabulary

Circle the word that is different and explain why.

1 artisan   architect   heir   merchant
2 abbey   palace   church   cathedral
3 window   wood   stone   glass
4 rats   horses   dogs   fleas
5 illness   disease   sickness   sick
6 Italy   Turkey   English   Britain

Now write a sentence using each word you circled.

INTERNET PROJECT

What was the Great Fire of 1666 like?

Click on **London's Burning** and then click on **Visit Our Special London's Burning** website. Divide the class into two groups. The first group can do a research project on **Themes**, and the other can do one on **People**. Prepare your project and present it to the class. Then play the **Great Fire of London Game** with your partner.

4 ACTIVITIES

Before you read

1 Vocabulary

Match the pictures (A-D) with the correct word (1-4).

1 carriage   2 factory   3 horse bus   4 slums

A

B

C

D

track 05

2 Listening

Listen to the first part of Chapter Four and choose the correct answer — A, B or C.

KET

1 During the Victorian Age
   A ☐ a lot of people went to London to work.
   B ☐ London was the only city to have big factories.
   C ☐ London was the world's second largest city.

2 The Queen's husband, Prince Albert
   A ☐ designed and built the Crystal Palace.
   B ☐ wrote a book about the Industrial Revolution.
   C ☐ organized the Great Exhibition of 1851.

3 Charles Dickens wrote about what he saw in the London streets
   A ☐ in the London newspaper.
   B ☐ in his novels.
   C ☐ in letters to Queen Victoria.

4 London had the first underground railway in the world
   A ☐ but it stopped working in the twentieth century.
   B ☐ but tickets were very expensive.
   C ☐ and Londoners called it 'the tube'.

CHAPTER **FOUR**

Dickens's London and the Early 20th Century

Many important events and changes took place during the Victorian Age and Dickens told us about them in his wonderful books.

A great novelist

track 05

The great British novelist Charles Dickens lived in London during Queen Victoria's reign (1837-1901) and most of his novels are set there. This period is known as the Victorian Age. Between 1837 and 1901 London's population grew from 2.5 million to 6.5 million and it was the world's largest city, a centre of industry and international trade. In the late 18th and early 19th centuries thousands of people came to work in London's factories because of the Industrial Revolution. After the invention of the railway in the 1830s even more people came to London.

An important event in Dickens's London was the Great Exhibition of 1851. During Queen Victoria's reign Britain became a very rich nation which made and exported [1] machines, ships,

1. **exported** : sold to other countries.

The Crystal Palace, Sydenham (about 1862).

cloth and other goods, and the Queen's husband, Prince Albert, organized the Great Exhibition to show Britain's goods to the world. People from all parts of the world came to show their goods too. The exhibition lasted 140 days and more than six million people visited it. It took place at Hyde Park, in a beautiful Crystal Palace made of iron [2] and glass, which was as big as four football fields.

London's streets

Dickens often walked the streets for hours and described what he saw in novels like *Oliver Twist*, *Bleak House* and *The Old Curiosity Shop*. Rich people, poor people, children, thieves, [3] criminals, horses and carriages all moved about in the same crowded, dirty streets. London's streets were noisy because

2. **iron**: a very strong metal used as a building material.
3. **thieves**: people who steal.

Dickens's London and the Early 20th Century

merchants shouted loudly to sell their goods. All kinds of rubbish was thrown in the streets and into the Thames and this caused health problems. At night most streets were dangerous because they were dark and there were many thieves and criminals. In 1888 the terrible murders [4] of Jack the Ripper took place in London's East End. Jack the Ripper was the name given to a man who murdered many young women and was never caught.

Like all big cities London had transportation problems. The horse bus was introduced in the 1830s and it carried about twenty-two passengers. In 1850 about a thousand horse buses an hour passed through London's central streets. Many of London's transportation problems were solved in 1863 with the world's first underground railway, called 'the tube' by Londoners. At first there were only a few stations but now it is the longest underground system in the world with eleven lines and 270 stations.

4. **murder** : violent killing of a person.

The Bayswater Omnibus (1895) by George William Joy.

London

Living and working conditions

London was a city of great differences. There were beautiful buildings and monuments near crowded slums where poor people lived in terrible conditions, like the East End and Soho. In the slums, houses were small, dirty and cold. There were no bathrooms, running water or heating. A big family usually lived in one room, often without a window.

Working conditions for adults and children were terrible. The working day in a factory was usually twelve hours long and the pay was very low. Poor children did not go to school because they had to work in factories, and they often did the most dangerous jobs. Some people had no work and no home and went to live in a workhouse. People in workhouses did unpleasant jobs in return for a little food and a place to live. The workhouses were sad places; Dickens wrote about them in *Oliver Twist*.

Dickens understood the problems of the poor because he had a difficult life when he was a child. He told his many readers about the great social problems of his city. Some Londoners decided to help and in 1865 William and Catherine Booth started the Salvation Army, which gave food and clothing to the poor. In 1867 Thomas Barnardo started a home for children who had no family and lived on the streets.

Dickens's London and the Early 20th Century

Applicants for Admission to a Casual Ward (1874) by Sir Lukes Fildes.

In Dickens's time the rich and the upper classes often went to live outside London in the countryside, where the air was clean. Their homes were big, warm and comfortable with lovely gardens, and their children had a good education.

Air and water

The air in London was dirty and unhealthy because smoke from the factories and fog created smog. [5] This caused many illnesses.

In Dickens's London people still drank water that came from the Thames, which was dirty and often caused terrible diseases like cholera. [6] In 1875 Sir Joseph Bazalgette, an engineer, built a big sewer [7] system for the city which made the water of the Thames much cleaner and safer.

---

5. **smog** : fog plus smoke from factories; very bad air.
6. **cholera** : a serious and often fatal disease caused by drinking dirty water.
7. **sewer** : an underground system that carries waste and rain water away.

London

Thanks to Dickens's novels many things changed during Queen Victoria's reign, because the government passed laws to improve the living and working conditions of the poor. But poverty remained a big problem during the 19th century.

The early 20th century

At the beginning of the 20th century London was still the largest city in the world, with a population of about six and a half million people, but in 1920 New York City became the largest with about ten million people.

During the years between the two World Wars (1918 to 1939) more people moved to the suburbs thanks to the car and the tube.

In World War II London was attacked from the air: the 'Blitz' was the name for the continued bombing of London and other

By the Thames. Children look over the railings by the banks of the Thames with Tower Bridge in the background.

1941: Bomb damage around St Paul's Cathedral.

parts of Britain by Nazi Germany. This took place between 7 September 1940 and 10 May 1941. During the Blitz most children were sent to the countryside because it was safer. The people who stayed in London had to hide in the tube during the bombings because it was the safest place.

London was bombed for fifty-seven consecutive [8] nights and around 41,000 people were killed and nearly 50,000 were badly hurt. A lot of important buildings, factories, ports and around one million homes were destroyed. Thousands of people were without a home and without a job.

After the war Britain's economy was weak, but it began to get better in the 1950s and 1960s. The London we see today is the result of a lot of hard work, building and improvement.

8. **consecutive** : one following the other.

4 ACTIVITIES

The text and **beyond**

KET **1** **Comprehension check**

Read the paragraph below and choose the best word (A, B or C) for each space (1-10). There is an example at the beginning (0).

Charles Dickens lived during the Victorian Age. Dickens's London was the world's (**0**)..C..... city. It was (**1**).......... important centre of industry and trade. The Industrial Revolution of the eighteenth and nineteenth century (**2**).......... thousands of workers to London.
The Great Exhibition of 1851 was organized (**3**).......... Prince Albert and showed Britain's goods to the world. More (**4**).......... six million people visited it. At that time London's streets were crowded, noisy and dirty. Dickens wrote (**5**).......... what he saw in his great novels, (**6**).......... *Oliver Twist and Bleak House*.
In 1863 the underground railway solved (**7**).......... of London's transportation problems and helped the city to grow. The poor lived in the slums and worked long hours in factories. Poor children could not go to school and (**8**).......... to work. The rich and the upper classes lived (**9**).......... London in big, comfortable homes with gardens.
London's air was dirty (**10**).......... smoke from the factories and fog created smog. In 1875 Sir Joseph Bazalgette built a sewer system which made the water of the Thames cleaner.
During the Blitz of World War II London was bombed (**11**).......... fifty-seven nights. The Blitz destroyed a big part of the city and (**12**).......... thousands of people.

ACTIVITIES 4

Smoke comes out of the famous chimneys of London's Battersea Power Station.

0	**A** larger	**B** bigger	**(C)** largest
1	**A** an	**B** a	**C** the
2	**A** took	**B** brought	**C** carried
3	**A** for	**B** to	**C** by
4	**A** than	**B** then	**C** of
5	**A** around	**B** about	**C** for
6	**A** such	**B** as	**C** like
7	**A** many	**B** much	**C** very
8	**A** must	**B** did	**C** had
9	**A** out	**B** outside	**C** away
10	**A** because	**B** why	**C** yet
11	**A** during	**B** for	**C** by
12	**A** died	**B** killing	**C** killed

2 Vocabulary

Find the opposites of these words in Chapter Four.

1 healthy ....
2 clean ....
3 wonderful ....
4 easy ....
5 safe ....
6 quiet ....
7 poor ....
8 strong ....

4 ACTIVITIES

KET 3 Vocabulary

A Read the definitions. What is the word for each one? The first letter is already there. There is one space for each other letter in the word. There is an example at the beginning (0).

0 A big show. e x h i b i t i o n
1 A strong building material. i _ _ _
2 People who steal. t _ _ _ _ _ _
3 Fog plus smoke from factories. s _ _ _
4 Sold to other countries. e _ _ _ _ _ _ _
5 An underground system that carries waste away. s _ _ _ _

B Write one sentence for each of the words above.

> **The clock is the largest four-faced ringing clock in the world.**
>
> **Largest** is the superlative of **large**.
> To form the superlative of one-syllable adjectives we use **the** and add **-est** to the end of the adjective (poor → **the poorest**).
> For words with two syllables or more we put **the most** in front of the adjective (difficult → **the most difficult**).
> Remember that some adjectives have irregular superlative forms. (good → **the best**, bad → **the worst**)

4 Superlatives

A Complete the table below with the superlative forms of the adjectives.

Adjective	Superlative	Adjective	Superlative
1 big	....	6 tall	....
2 rich	....	7 crowded	....
3 dangerous	....	8 bad	....
4 great	....	9 fast	....
5 dirty	....	10 large	....

ACTIVITIES 4

B Complete the sentences using some of the superlative adjectives on page 46.

1. By the beginning of the twentieth century London was the .... city in the world.
2. Poor people had the .... working and living conditions.
3. Jack the Ripper was the .... criminal of Victorian London.
4. The .... people had big, comfortable homes in the countryside.
5. The Great Exhibition was one of the .... exhibitions of the nineteenth century.

INTERNET PROJECT

Let's find out more about children in the Victorian Age!
Dickens wrote about children in the Victorian Age in his wonderful novels. Divide the class into three groups and each one can do a brief research project on Work, School and Play. Present it to the class
Which group had the most interesting report and why?
Compare the conditions of Victorian children with children of today.

London and Its Writers

Perhaps no other city has such a rich literary [1] history as London. Nowhere else in the world is there a place like Poets' Corner in Westminster Abbey. Twenty-eight famous British writers are buried there and more than fifty are remembered with a memorial plaque. Geoffrey Chaucer, author of *The Canterbury Tales*, was the first writer buried there in 1400.

Let's take a look at some of the famous writers who lived and worked in London.

Writers of the Elizabethan Age

William Shakespeare probably arrived in London in 1588 and began writing his great plays. He wrote most of them between 1590 to 1611. He joined the Lord Chamberlain's Men acting company in 1594 and worked as an actor and playwright. At first the acting company worked at The Theatre and The Curtain, two theatres north of the Thames. Shakespeare's plays were very popular and in 1599 he and the Lord Chamberlain's Men decided to build their own theatre, The Globe, in Southwark. During his life Shakespeare wrote 38 plays – comedies, tragedies and histories – and many poems. During Shakespeare's time there were other important writers who lived and worked in London. In 1587 Christopher Marlowe went to

1. **literary**: about literature.

Poets' Corner, Westminster Abbey.

London to work as a playwright and poet. His most famous play was *Doctor Faustus*.

Ben Jonson was another important playwright who lived in London at the same time as Shakespeare and Marlowe. His best known plays are *Volpone* and *The Alchemist*. He is buried standing up in Poets' Corner!

The Romantics in London

William Wordsworth was one of England's first Romantic poets. He went to London in 1791 and stayed in Cheapside, near St Paul's Cathedral. He did not stay in London for a long time but he liked it very much. He often went to listen to the discussions in Parliament and took walks around the city. His famous poem 'Composed Upon Westminster Bridge, September 3rd, 1802' speaks of the ships, towers and buildings he sees from the bridge. The first line of the poem says: 'Earth has nothing to show more fair.' [2]

At the end of the eighteenth and beginning of the nineteenth century three important Romantic poets were part of London's literary scene: Lord Byron, Percy Bysshe Shelley and John Keats.

John Keats was born in London in 1795. As a young man he started studying medicine but he liked literature more, so he decided to become a poet. He lived in a house in Hampstead in north London from 1818 to 1820. During these two years he wrote 'Ode to a Nightingale' and many other poems. He also fell in love with Fanny Brawne, the girl who lived next door; his poem 'Bright Star' is about when he met Fanny. Keats had health problems and travelled to Italy where the weather was warmer. He liked living in Italy but his health did not improve. He died in Rome at the young age of 26. Today Keats's house in Hampstead is a museum which you can visit.

George Gordon Byron, better known as Lord Byron, was born in London in 1797. In 1811 he had a seat in Parliament, in the House of Lords. Lord Byron was an unusual man with an adventurous life style and London newspapers and magazines often wrote about him. They wrote about him so much that he left England and visited several European countries, where he continued writing his poems. His most famous work is the long poem *Don Juan*.

Percy Bysshe Shelley was born in 1792. He went to Eton School, the most famous in England but he didn't like it. He didn't like Oxford University either. He was different from the other students and

2. **fair** : beautiful.

wanted to be a poet. When Shelley met Byron in London they became good friends because they had the same ideas about art, poetry, government and society. They did not like British society and decided to leave. In 1816 Byron, Shelley and his girlfriend Mary Wollstonecraft stayed together near Lake Geneva in Switzerland, where Mary wrote her famous novel *Frankenstein* (1818). Shelley's best-known works are the poems 'To a Skylark' and 'Ode to the West Wind' and the poetic play *Prometheus Unbound*.

London's Victorian writers

Charles Dickens was born in Portsmouth in 1812. When he was twelve years old his family became poor and he had to leave school and go to work in a factory in London. He never forgot this terrible experience and wrote about the problems of the poor in Victorian London in his novels.

Dickens's first novel, *The Pickwick Papers* (1836), was published in parts and was very successful. Many of his other works were published week by week or month by month in London magazines before they became books. Dickens and his family lived in different houses in London, but the most

Charles Dickens (19th century) by William Powell Frith.

famous was at 48 Doughty Street, which is now the Dickens House Museum. Some of his best known novels were written there: *The Pickwick Papers*, *Oliver Twist* and *Nicholas Nickleby*.

Sherlock Holmes Museum in Baker Street.

Sir Arthur Conan Doyle was born in Scotland in 1859 and studied medicine at Edinburgh University. He became an eye doctor and started working in London. But he had very few patients and so he started writing his first novel, *A Study in Scarlet*, which was the first Sherlock Holmes story. He wrote stories about the clever London detective for a popular monthly magazine called *The Strand*, and they were a great success. Doyle created one of the world's most famous detectives, and he continued writing stories about him until 1927. Doyle also wrote science fiction (*The Lost World*) and historical novels. Today you can visit the Sherlock Holmes Museum at 221B Baker Street in London.

The Irish writer Oscar Wilde became one of the most successful playwrights in late Victorian London. His plays *The Importance of Being Earnest*, *Lady Windermere's Fan* and *An Ideal Husband* were very entertaining and audiences loved them. Wilde became famous

and had an exciting social life in London. Newspapers and magazines always wrote about him. In 1890-91 he published his only novel, *The Picture of Dorian Gray*. He also wrote poems and short stories for adults and children. You can see Oscar Wilde's London home at 34 Tite Street in Chelsea.

J. M. Barrie was a Scottish writer who worked in London in the 1890s. He was a friend of Sir Arthur Conan Doyle and became famous with his wonderful play *Peter Pan*, which had its first performance in London in 1904. His play later became a popular novel. There are several films, musicals and plays about Peter Pan, the boy who did not want to grow up. In Kensington Gardens in London you can see a life-size statue of Peter Pan.

The Bloomsbury Group was a group of friends who lived in the area of Bloomsbury Square, near the British Museum, during the first half of the twentieth century. They were writers, critics, artists, painters and philosophers who had an unusual life style. Famous writers like Virginia Woolf and E.M. Forster were part of the Bloomsbury Group which was important in modern literature.

1 Answer the following questions.

1. Who were the important writers of the Elizabethan Age?
2. Who wrote 'Composed Upon Westminster Bridge, September 3rd, 1802', and what is it about?
3. Where did John Keats live in London?
4. Why did Lord Byron and Shelley become good friends?
5. Where did Charles Dickens write his first novel?
6. Who did Sir Arthur Conan Doyle write about?
7. Who was the most famous playwright in late Victorian London?
8. Why was the Bloomsbury Group important?

INTERNET PROJECT

Let's visit two important homes: Charles Dickens's and Sherlock Holmes's!

Work with a partner and visit the two homes. Take the virtual tour of Charles Dickens's Museum House, and then take the museum tour and video tour of Sherlock Holmes's Museum House. Which house did you like more and why?

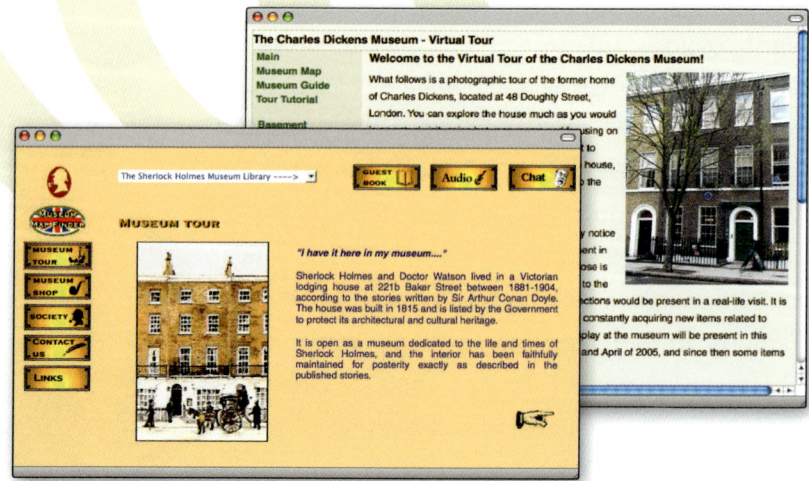

CHAPTER FIVE

Westminster Today

Many of London's most important historic buildings are in Westminster, the centre of government.

Westminster and Whitehall

track 06

Westminster is about a mile west of the City. For centuries Westminster was the political and religious centre, and the City was London's business centre. Today Westminster is still the centre of government.

Westminster Hall was built in 1099 by the son of William the Conqueror and is one of Europe's largest medieval halls. It was part of the medieval Westminster Palace, which was destroyed by a fire in 1834. The Houses of Parliament that we see today were built in the 19th century after the fire. Today the House of Commons and the House of Lords meet at the Houses of Parliament, also known as the New Palace of Westminster.

The Big Ben clock tower, built at the same time as the New Palace of Westminster, rises above the Houses of Parliament and is one of London's most famous symbols. The clock is the largest

Westminster Palace seen through the London Eye.

four-faced ringing clock in the world. Some people think that Big Ben is the name of the clock on the tower, but this is not true. Big Ben is the name of the big 13-ton bell that rings every quarter of an hour.

Victoria Tower is at the west end of the Houses of Parliament. It is the entrance used by the King or Queen when he or she opens a new session of government. The British flag — the correct name is 'the Union Flag' but it is often called 'the Union Jack' — flies from the tower when Parliament meets. Outside the Houses of Parliament in the old Palace Yard you can see a beautiful statue [1] of King Richard I, known as Richard the Lionheart, on his horse.

Near the Houses of Parliament is Westminster Bridge with its excellent views along the Thames. Near the bridge there is

1. statue :

Westminster Today

Westminster Pier, where you can catch a boat for a wonderful ride on the Thames. One of the best ways to see London is from the river.

The most historic religious building in Britain is Westminster Abbey, a beautiful church across the street from the Houses of Parliament. It was started in the seventh century. William the Conqueror was crowned [2] King of England in the Abbey on Christmas Day 1066. Through the centuries monarchs of England and Britain were crowned and buried [3] here. They are still crowned here.

Poets' Corner in the Abbey is a special place where Britain's greatest writers — novelists, poets and playwrights — are either buried or remembered with a memorial plaque. [4] Chaucer, Spenser, Dickens, Kipling and many other great writers are buried in Poets' Corner. Memorial plaques remember great people who are buried in other places, such as William Shakespeare, the Brontë sisters, Oscar Wilde and others. Great

Westminster Abbey.

2. **crowned** : made king.
3. **buried** : when the body of a dead person is put under the ground.
4. **memorial plaque** : a sign that remembers a famous person or event.

scientists like Isaac Newton and Charles Darwin and famous military men like Lord Nelson are buried in other parts of the Abbey.

If you walk along Whitehall you will see Britain's most important government offices and buildings: the Treasury, the Foreign and Commonwealth Office, the Banqueting House, Horse Guards Parade and the Prime Minster's famous residence at number 10 Downing Street. Near the Treasury are the Cabinet War Rooms, secret underground rooms used by Sir Winston Churchill and military leaders during World War II (1939-45). Important military plans were decided there and you can still see Churchill's office (where he also slept), and the same phones, maps and furniture used during the war years.

Buckingham Palace

Queen Victoria was the first monarch who lived at Buckingham Palace — she moved here in 1837, when she became queen — and this palace is now the official London residence of the British

Buckingham Palace.

monarch. The monarch does not own the palace; it belongs to the British state. Most of the palace was built between 1820 and 1837, and it has six hundred rooms. The beautiful State Ballroom is the largest room at Buckingham Palace and is used for special events. The palace has an important Picture Gallery with famous paintings by artists like Rembrandt, Rubens and Van Dyck.

Buckingham Palace is open to the public during the months of August and September, when the Royal Family is away for the summer. If you're interested in horses and carriages, you can visit the Royal Mews, [5] which is next to the palace. Here you can see the monarch's horses and the Gold State Coach, which was built for King George III in 1762. This coach is still used by the monarch on important occasions.

The Changing of the Guard.

Most visitors want to see the Changing of the Guard, which takes place in front of Buckingham Palace and lasts forty minutes. The guards are soldiers who protect the monarch. This colourful event, when a new group of soldiers arrives and the previous group leaves, takes place at 11.30 every morning from April to July, and every other morning at the same time from August to March.

5. **mews** : an old word for a street with stables for horses.

London

The Mall is a lovely tree-lined street which goes from Buckingham Palace to Trafalgar Square. The monarch rides along the Mall in the Gold State Coach, with more than a hundred soldiers on horses, when she/he leaves Buckingham Palace for the State Opening of Parliament in autumn.

Along one side of The Mall you can see beautiful historic buildings and houses, such as St James's Palace, once the home of King Henry VIII, Marlborough House, Clarence House and Lancaster House. St James's Park, about which you will read more on page 77, is on the other side of the Mall.

St James's Palace.

ACTIVITIES 5

The text and **beyond**

1 Comprehension check

Are these sentences 'Right' (A) or 'Wrong' (B)? If there is not enough information to answer 'Right' or 'Wrong', choose 'Doesn't say' (C). There is an example at the beginning (0).

		A	B	C
0	Westminster has an area of about a square mile.			✓
1	Westminster Hall was built in the eleventh century.			
2	Big Ben is the name of the largest four-faced ringing clock in the world.			
3	The House of Commons and the House of Lords meet every week.			
4	William the Conqueror built Westminster Abbey in 1066.			
5	Kings and queens are not buried in Poets' Corner in Westminster Abbey.			
6	Queen Victoria was the last queen to live in Buckingham Palace.			
7	Tourists cannot visit Buckingham Palace during the winter.			
8	It takes forty minutes to watch the Changing of the Guard.			
9	The Mall connects Westminster to Whitehall.			
10	St James Palace is on The Mall.			

5 ACTIVITIES

2 Prepositions

Use the prepositions below to complete the sentences. You can use them more than once.

> for   with   during   at   on   through

1   When you walk .... Whitehall you can see all the important government buildings.
2   The British flag flies .... the tower when Parliament meets.
3   A boat ride .... the Thames is a great way to see London.
4   The Prime Minister lives .... number 10 Downing Street.
5   The Gold State Coach was built .... King George III.
6   The Cabinet War Rooms were used .... World War II.
7   Richard is sitting .... his horse.
8   Big Ben always rings .... noon.
9   Some writers in Poets' Corner are remembered .... a memorial plaque.

T: GRADE 3

3 Speaking: places in the local area

Westminster, Whitehall, Buckingham Palace and The Mall are places of interest in London. What are your favourite places of interest in your town or city? Tell the class about them and use these questions to help you.

1   Describe one of your favourite places. What do you like about it?
2   How often do you visit it?
3   What do you do when you're there?
4   Do you go alone or with your friends?
5   How do you get there?

ACTIVITIES **5**

4 **Question words**
We use words like *when, why, how, where, what, who* to make questions. Look at the questions and answers below. Choose the correct word from those above and complete the questions (1-6). Then find the correct answers (A-F)

1 .... is Westminster? ....
2 .... can you see on The Mall? ....
3 .... many faces does the clock on the Big Ben clock tower have? ....
4 .... were the Houses of Parliament rebuilt in the nineteenth century? ....
5 .... built Westminster Hall? ....
6 .... did Sir Winston Churchill work in the Cabinet War Rooms? ....

A ☐ Because a fire destroyed the Palace of Westminster in 1835.
B ☐ St James Palace, Marlborough House, Clarence House and Lancaster House.
C ☐ During World War II.
D ☐ It has four faces.
E ☐ The son of William the Conqueror.
F ☐ It is about a mile west of the City.

6 ACTIVITIES

Before you read

1 Vocabulary
Match the words (1-3) to the pictures (A-C).

1 escalator
2 neon lights
3 hoardings

2 Listening

track 07

KET

Listen to part of Chapter Six. Choose the correct answers — A, B or C.

1 Who was Horatio Nelson?
   A the Mayor of Oslo
   B a commander during World War II
   C a British commander

2 Where can you find most of London's theatres?
   A in the West End
   B in Trafalgar Square
   C near St Martin-in-the Fields church

3 Where can you find many of London's department stores?
   A Shaftesbury Avenue
   B Oxford Street and Knightsbridge
   C Westminster

4 What were customers afraid of in the late 1800s?
   A the lift
   B the high prices
   C the escalator

5 How did Robert Baker make a lot of money?
   A He built big houses for the rich.
   B He founded a department store.
   C He made and sold big collars for men.

64

CHAPTER **SIX**

The West End

The West End is an exciting part of London. It is home to London's finest museums, theatres, art galleries, shops, restaurants and hotels.

Trafalgar Square and the West End

 track 07

Visitors often ask, 'Where is the centre of London?' That's a difficult question to answer because London has many centres. Trafalgar Square is often called the heart of London because it connects the political area of Westminster to the rest of West London.

Lord Nelson's column stands in the centre of this beautiful square. It is a memorial to the great British commander Horatio Nelson and the famous Battle of Trafalgar, off the southwest of Spain, in 1805. Lord Nelson won the sea battle at Trafalgar against the French and Spanish, but he himself was killed. Every year there is a Christmas ceremony in Trafalgar Square. The city of Oslo in Norway sends a tall Christmas tree to thank Britain for its help during World War II and the Mayor of Oslo comes to London to light the tree.

On the north side of the square is the National Gallery, about

Trafalgar Square and Nelson's Column.

which you will read more on page 79, and to the east is the church of St Martin-in-the-Fields.

To the north and west of Trafalgar Square is the West End, which is London's shopping and entertainment area. The West End goes from Temple Bar along the River Thames to Chelsea and Knightbridge in the west, and to Bloomsbury and Marylebone Road in the north.

Most of London's best residential and commercial areas are in the West End: fine shops, restaurants, hotels, famous theatres, museums and art galleries. Oxford Street is a two-mile long shopping area with large department stores like Selfridge's, John Lewis and Marks and Spencer. Regent Street is nearby and you can visit Hamley's, the largest toy shop in the world. Regent Street is part of the original Roman road from London to Oxford.

Great Britain's biggest department store is in Knightsbridge. It was founded in 1834 by Charles Henry Harrod and in 1898 it had the world's first escalator for its customers. The first customers who took the escalator were afraid of it! Today

Harrods is an amazing place with over 330 departments that sell just about everything you can think of. And if you get hungry while shopping there are twenty-six fine eating places inside the department store. The Food Hall at Harrods has special food and sweets from all over the world and is a lot of fun to visit.

London is the theatre capital of the world and most of its best theatres are in the West End or on Shaftesbury Avenue, which is often called 'Theatreland'. There are always many fine plays and musicals to choose from.

Soho and Mayfair district, Oxford Street.

Piccadilly rush hour.

London

Piccadilly is an important street that goes from Hyde Park Corner to the famous Piccadilly Circus. Its name comes from 'Piccadilly Hall', a name given to house built by Robert Baker in the seventeenth century. Baker made and sold *piccadils* — big collars that were the fashion for men at that time. He made a lot of money and built a big house, which people called 'Piccadilly Hall'. The house is no longer there, but it gave its name to Piccadilly.

One of Britain's best and oldest department stores is Fortnum and Masons at 181 Piccadilly. It was founded in 1707 and sells fine food, tea, coffee, sweets and many other products. You can do more shopping at the beautiful Piccadilly Arcade, with its sixteen shops and at the Burlington and Royal Opera Arcades.

Piccadilly Circus and Soho

Piccadilly Circus is a big public space built in 1819. The word 'circus' here comes from the Latin word for circle, and it means a big open space where people meet. There are always a lot of tourists and traffic in the Circus, with its big neon signs. Young people like sitting and relaxing around the Shaftesbury memorial fountain with the statue known as Eros, the god of love. Not far from the Circus is Carnaby Street,

Carnaby Street.

which was a fashion centre for young people in the 1960s; today it is a big tourist attraction.

Soho is an area north of Piccadilly Circus near Oxford Street. It attracted many foreigners, artists and writers in the past — Karl Marx lived here for five years and today there are many good, inexpensive places to eat. Until 1536 it was part of King Henry VIII's royal park for the Palace of Whitehall. People think that the word 'soho' was a hunting call ('So-ho! So-ho! There goes the fox!').

Old Compton Road is the heart of Soho and here you can find French, Italian and Middle Eastern food shops, coffee shops and restaurants. The musician Mozart lived on Frith Street when he was a child in 1764. In Robert Louis Stevenson's novel *The Strange Case of Dr Jekyll and Mr Hyde,* Dr Henry Jekyll rented rooms for Edward Hyde in Soho.

Soho, Chinatown.

London's Chinatown is on Gerrard Street in Soho, where there are Chinese restaurants and shops. Signs are written in Chinese with the English translation. Towards the end of January or the beginning of February thousands of people watch the colourful Chinese New Year parade in Chinatown.

Charing Cross Road divides Soho from Covent Garden and is famous for its many bookshops. Here you can find all kinds of new and used books. Foyle's on Charing Cross Road is London's largest bookshop and a fun place to visit.

Covent Garden and The Strand

Covent Garden's old name was Convent Garden because the gardens of a medieval convent [1] were located there. In 1630 the great architect Inigo Jones created Covent Garden Piazza, the first Italian-style square in London. For centuries Covent Garden was London's biggest fruit, vegetable and flower market, but in 1974 the market moved away. In George Bernard Shaw's play *Pygmalion* (1913) the opening scenes take place in the market at Covent Garden.

In 1980 Covent Garden became a modern shopping centre and tourist attraction with shops, eating places, street performers and musicians. The famous Royal Opera House and the Royal Ballet are at Covent Garden. The Theatre Royal in Drury Lane is London's oldest indoor theatre; it was built in 1663. It is known as a haunted [2] theatre because people say that ghosts

Covent Garden entrance.

1. **convent** : a place where religious people live.
2. **haunted** : with ghosts.

The West End

of actors live there... but they bring good luck to actors who see them!

The Strand is a famous street that starts at Trafalgar Square. It runs east and becomes Fleet Street at Temple Bar, where the City begins. The name Strand comes from the old English word 'river bank' or 'shore', because in the Middle Ages the street was next to the River Thames. It connected the City and the Palace of Westminster. Between 1865 and 1870 the Victoria Embankment [3] was built so the Strand was further away

Covent Garden Market.

3. **Victoria Embankment** : a road and walkway next to the River Thames.

from the river. The Strand was the centre of Victorian theatres and nightlife, but only a few theatres remain today.

The largest street carnival in Europe takes place every year at Notting Hill to the west of the West End, during the last weekend of August. The Notting Hill Carnival is a three-day multi-cultural [4] event and more than a million people go and enjoy the traditional Caribbean music, dancing, food and costumes.

People in costumes at Notting Hill Gate's annual carnival.

4. **multi-cultural** : where there are people of different races and cultures.

ACTIVITIES 6

The text and **beyond**

1 Comprehension check
Complete the following sentences (1-9). Choose from the endings A-J. There is one extra sentence.

1 Lord Nelson won .....
2 Great Britain helped Norway .....
3 Most of London's famous theatres .....
4 The largest department store in Britain .....
5 The Shaftesbury memorial fountain .....
6 In the past Soho .....
7 Covent Garden Piazza was the first .....
8 In the Victorian Age the Strand .....
9 The Notting Hill Carnival .....

A is in Knightsbridge.
B was the centre of Victorian theatres.
C the old name of Piccadilly.
D the Battle of Trafalgar in 1805.
E Italian-style square in London.
F attracted many foreigners and artists.
G during World War II.
H are in the West End or near Shaftesbury Avenue.
I is a big multi-cultural event in West London.
J is in Piccadilly Circus.

6 ACTIVITIES

2 Listening

You will hear some tourist information about Buckingham Palace. Listen and complete questions 1-6.

BUCKINGHAM PALACE
Hours: (1) ....
Ticket price for students: (2) ....
Ticket price for a family: (3) ....
Tube stations: (4) ....
You can see: (5) ....
Please don't bring: (6) ....

3 Writing

Complete these letters. Write ONE word for each space. There is an example at the beginning. (0).

Dear Kate,
Thanks (0) ...for... the lovely postcard from London with the red double-decker buses. I showed it (1).......... my brother Matt and now he wants to go. London looks (2).......... a great city with a lot of fun things to do. My parents said that if Matt and (3).......... do well at school, they will take (4).......... to London next summer.
Call me when you get back!
Susan

ACTIVITIES 6

Dear Susan,

London (5).......... wonderful! There (6).......... many fun things to do every day.
Yesterday morning we took a boat ride (7).......... the Thames. Yesterday in the afternoon we (8).......... to the Globe Theatre to see Shakespeare's Romeo and Juliet and we loved it. Today we're (9).......... to visit the Tower of London. Tomorrow mom and I are going to shop, but (10).......... dad isn't very happy about this.
See you soon!
Kate

INTERNET PROJECT

Let's meet the ghosts at Drury Lane!

People think the Theatre Royal Drury Lane is haunted. Work with a partner and read about what people say about the ghosts at the Theatre Royal, Drury Lane.

What do you think? Are there ghosts at the theatre? What does your class say? What does your teacher say?

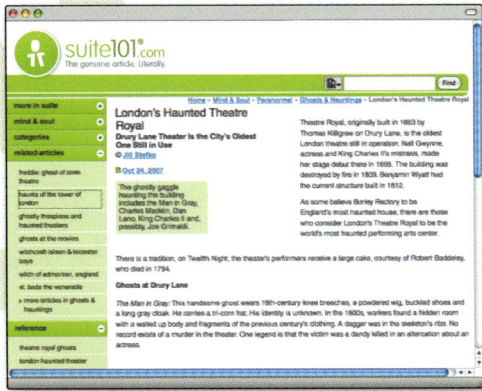

75

DOSSIER

London's Parks and Museums

Parks

London is one the greenest big cities in the world. Everywhere you go there is always a park or garden. There are 387 parks in Greater London! Most of these green open spaces were once the parks of royal homes and palaces. Now these lovely parks belong to the people, and in many parks you can rent a deck chair [1] and sit on the grass and enjoy the sun or read a book.

Hyde Park is the best-known of the great royal parks with more than 4,000 trees. It was first owned by the monks [2] of Westminster Abbey and then by King Henry VIII, who went hunting there. In the 1600s it was opened to the public and in 1665, during the Great Plague, many people left the City and went to stay in Hyde Park. The Serpentine Lake is a big attraction because you can swim in it all year long or you can rent a boat. You can also go biking or riding in the park. On Sundays you can listen to people at Speakers' Corner, where anyone can talk about any subject. In the summer many fun events take place in the park. Famous singers and bands often perform here.

To the west of Hyde Park are Kensington Gardens. They are the grounds [3] of Kensington Palace, which was the also the home of

1. **deck chair** :
2. **monks** :
3. **grounds** : the land around a building.

Diana, Princess of Wales. These gardens have beautiful fountains and statues and lots of colourful flowers and plants. The famous statue of Peter Pan is here and it is a big attraction for everyone who loves the wonderful story. At the far end of the park is the Round Pond, where children (and adults!) can play with model boats.

Going east we find one of London's oldest royal parks, St James's Park. In 1532 King Henry VIII bought the land where the park is today. In 1603 King James I created a park where he kept wild animals like camels, elephants and birds. In the 1660s King Charles II asked a French artist to redesign [4] the park, which was later opened to the public. There is a large lake with Duck Island, where different kinds of ducks and birds live. Every afternoon at 2.30 the pelicans [5] are given fresh fish to eat and it is fun to watch them. On summer weekends you can listen to concerts in the park. All around the park you can see some

4. **redesign** : to design again.   5. **pelicans** :

of the country's most famous places: Buckingham Palace, The Mall and Whitehall. Regent's Park is north of Oxford Street and it has an Inner and Outer Ring. Within the Inner Ring are the lovely Queen Mary's Gardens and the Open Air Theatre where Shakespeare's plays are performed in the summer. The London Zoo, with over 750 kinds of animals, is in the Outer Ring.

Museums

There are more than 240 museums in London and most of them are free. Some are small and others are very large, and they are all fun to visit. Let's take a look at the most important ones.

The British Museum is one of the largest and most important museums in the world. It has more than seven million objects from all over the world: Ancient Egypt, Ancient Greece and Rome, the Americas, Europe, Asia and the Middle East. These objects tell the story of human culture from its beginning to the present. For example, in the Egyptian Sculpture section you can see the famous Rosetta Stone, which was the key to reading ancient Egyptian writing. And in the Greek section you can see the beautiful Parthenon Sculptures from the Acropolis in Athens.

The museum was opened to the public in 1759. During the years many important objects were added to the collections.

The centre of the museum was redesigned by the famous British architect Sir Norman Foster, and in 2000 it became the beautiful Great Court with a glass and steel roof, which surrounds the original Reading Room. It is the largest covered open space in Europe – it is bigger than a football field!

The Great Court in British Museum.

The Natural History Museum is the largest and most important natural history museum in the world. It has more than 70 million specimens: [6] animals, insects, birds, plants, rocks and minerals. The museum is famous for its skeletons of dinosaurs and other big mammals, and its section on biodiversity. The museum opened in 1881 but its history goes back to the late 1700s, when Captain Cook brought back many unusual specimens from his trips to the South Pacific. The museum is on Exhibition Road in South Kensington near two other famous museums, the Science Museum and the Victoria and Albert Museum. This area is often called 'Museum Mile'.

The National Gallery is the biggest building on Trafalgar Square. It was founded in 1924 and has a world famous collection of over 2,300 paintings from the mid-13th century to 1900. Almost every important artist in the world is represented in

6. **specimen** : a plant or animal which is the example of a particular species.

Natural History Museum: diplodocus skeleton.

the wonderful collection – from medieval painters, to the great Renaissance artists, to the 19th- century impressionists.

If you want to find out more about London's history from the prehistoric days up to now, go to the Museum of London in the City. See what prehistoric London was like in the London Before London exhibit, which goes back to the year 450,000 BCE!

There is an excellent simulation [7] of the Great Fire of 1666, where you can see what happened during the fire and how people tried to put it out. You can also hear about different people's adventures during the disaster. Near the museum you can see the old Roman city wall.

7. **simulation** : something that shows you how the real thing was.

1) Are these sentences true (T) or false (F)? Correct the false ones.

		T	F
1	Most of the parks in London belong to the Royal family.	☐	☐
2	The Serpentine Lake is in Hyde Park.	☐	☐
3	Speakers' Corner is near the statue of Peter Pan.	☐	☐
4	Wild animals lived in St James's Park in the early 1600s.	☐	☐
5	Only pelicans live on Duck Island.	☐	☐
6	You can see a big collection of paintings at the British Museum.	☐	☐
7	The largest covered open space in Europe is inside the British Museum.	☐	☐
8	Many of Captain Cook's unusual specimens are at the Natural History Museum.	☐	☐

INTERNET PROJECT

Let's visit the Tate Online!

Tate Britain is a world famous gallery of British art founded in 1897 on Millbank in London. It is one of the four Tate galleries in Great Britain: Tate Modern, Tate Liverpool and Tate St Ives. Divide the class into two groups; one can do research and a report on Tate Britain and the other can do the same on Tate Modern.
In your report remember to include:
- visitor information
- the collections
- the special exhibitions
- any other interesting news

Present your report to the class. Did you recognize any of the paintings? If so, which ones? Which Tate did you like best and why?

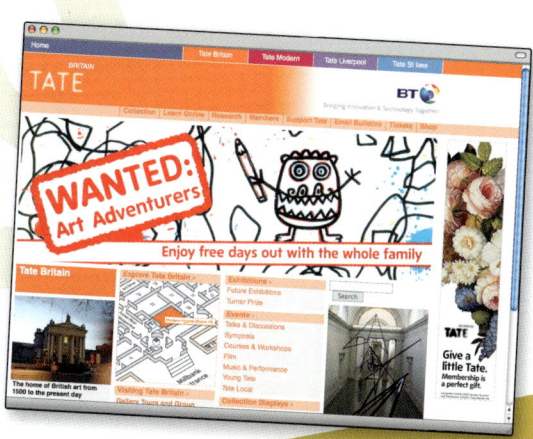

7 ACTIVITIES

Before you read

  Listening

 Listen to part of Chapter Seven. Choose the correct answer — A, B or C.

1 What is the Temple Bar Memorial?
   - A ☐ It is a monument built by the Romans two thousand years ago.
   - B ☐ It is a separate city within London.
   - C ☐ It is a bronze statue of a dragon.

2 What is the smallest British city?
   - A ☐ St David's.
   - B ☐ The City.
   - C ☐ Londinium.

3 How many people live in the Square Mile?
   - A ☐ 8,000.
   - B ☐ 400,000.
   - C ☐ 500.

4 What is the biggest performing arts centre in Europe?
   - A ☐ The Royal Exchange.
   - B ☐ The Barbican Centre.
   - C ☐ The Guildhall.

5 Where was the first newspaper published?
   - A ☐ On Cheapside Street.
   - B ☐ At Lloyd's of London.
   - C ☐ On Fleet Street.

6 What did William the Conqueror build in 1078?
   - A ☐ The medieval Guildhall.
   - B ☐ Temple Church.
   - C ☐ The White Tower.

CHAPTER **SEVEN**

The City and Beyond

The Romans founded Londinium, where the City stands today. London's City is one of the world most interesting square miles.

The statue of a bronze [1] dragon on Fleet Street is the entrance to the City of London. It is known as the Temple Bar Memorial. This is where the Romans founded Londinium almost two thousand years ago. The City covers only about 2.6 sq km (about 1 sq mile) and it is often called the Square Mile. It is a separate city with its own laws, police force and mayor. [2] It is the second smallest British city in both population and size after St David's in Wales.

Today the City is one of the world's most important business and financial centres, with the Royal Exchange, the London Stock Exchange, Lloyd's of London, the Bank of England and over 500 other banks. There are thousands of international offices in the many tall, modern buildings of the City. Over 400,000 people work within the Square Mile during weekdays and it is a

track 09

1. **bronze** : a metal.
2. **mayor** : the head of a town or city.

London

crowded, noisy place. In the City there is an open space known as The Bank which is particularly busy and crowded during weekdays. At the weekends there are very few people in the streets because only about 8,000 people live there.

The Barbican Centre is a very big complex of buildings, towers, garages and walkways. It was built in the 1970s and most Londoners don't like the way it looks. It is the largest performing arts centre in Europe and home to two symphony orchestras, a theatre, an art gallery, a cinema and the excellent Museum of London.

Fleet Street was once a road between the City and Westminster. Then it became the centre of the publishing and newspaper business for centuries. William Caxton was the first person to introduce the printing press to England and in the early 1500s printers and publishers opened their shops on Fleet Street. In 1702 *The Daily Courant* was the first newspaper published on Fleet Street. During the 1980s *The Times* and other important newspapers moved to the Docklands in the East End.

The terrible Blitz of World War II destroyed many of the beautiful old buildings in the City. Luckily the medieval Guildhall near Cheapside and Basinghall Streets and some important old

churches like Temple Church are still standing. One of the most interesting things to see in the City is St Paul's Cathedral. Its huge dome [3] is 110 metres high and is the second tallest dome in the world. If you climb to the top of the dome you'll get a wonderful view of London.

3. **dome** : a round roof.

London

The City's oldest building is the historic White Tower, which was built by William the Conqueror in 1078. The White Tower is part of a group of buildings constructed during the 13th and 14th centuries and surrounded by two big walls and other towers. The whole group of buildings and towers is called the Tower of London.

The Tower of London.

The Tower has a long, interesting history. It was a fortress, a royal palace and a prison. Executions of important prisoners took place on Tower Green, including Anne Boleyn and Catherine Howard (two of Henry VIII's six wives) and Lady Jane Grey (who was Queen for just ten days in 1553). But executions of ordinary prisoners took place outside the Tower. People say that the Tower is the most haunted building in England, with the ghosts

The City and Beyond

of Anne Boleyn, Lady Jane Grey, the Princes in the Tower and others. The Tower of London is mentioned in William Shakespeare's play *Richard III*.

Today thirty-five Yeomen Warders — also known as 'Beefeaters' — in their traditional uniforms are the guards and tour guides of the Tower. Thousands of tourists visit the Tower of London every day and there is always a long queue to see the Crown Jewels of the Royal family, which are kept in the Jewel House Tower.

A raven.

No one knows when the ravens came to the Tower of London, but an old legend says that if the ravens leave, the kingdom will fall. Today eight ravens live there, and each one has a name. No one wants the ravens to leave, so some feathers are taken from

Yeoman Warders, also known as Beefeaters, before they start work at the Tower of London.

London

their wings so that they can't fly and they are looked after by the Ravenmaster, who is one of the Yeomen. At night they sleep in their cages and during the day they are free to move around.

Tower Bridge, very near the Tower of London, is a symbol of London and is one of the several bridges that cross the Thames. It was built during the Victorian Age in 1894, when London was a busy port. At that time, the central part of the bridge opened several times a day for ships to pass. Today the bridge opens only a couple of times a week, but it is still a big tourist attraction. You can get great views of London from the top of the two towers and from the walkway that connects them.

There are many more places to see and things to do in this wonderful city but the best thing to do is to *go and visit*!

Tower Bridge.

ACTIVITIES 7

INTERNET PROJECT

Let's visit Tower Bridge!

Tower Bridge is an amazing structure with a wonderful view of London. Go to the website, click on Photo Gallery and enjoy the great pictures. Discuss them with your partner.

7 ACTIVITIES

The text and **beyond**

KET **1 Comprehension check**

Choose the correct answer — A, B or C.

1 The Temple Bar Memorial is
   A ☐ the town hall of the City.
   B ☐ the entrance to the City.
   C ☐ a bronze statue of a horse.

2 More than 400,000 people
   A ☐ go to London to work every day.
   B ☐ live in the City.
   C ☐ work in the City on weekdays.

3 In the past Fleet Street
   A ☐ was the home of printers and publishers.
   B ☐ was the home of the Barbican Centre.
   C ☐ was the home of Christopher Wren.

4 The medieval Guildhall and St Paul's Cathedral
   A ☐ were designed by Christopher Wren.
   B ☐ are haunted buildings.
   C ☐ were not destroyed in the Blitz.

5 The Tower of London
   A ☐ is in the centre of the Square Mile.
   B ☐ is a group of buildings and towers.
   C ☐ is the tallest part of Tower Bridge.

6 In the past executions of important prisoners
   A ☐ took place at The Bank.
   B ☐ took place at Buckingham Palace.
   C ☐ took place on Tower Green.

ACTIVITIES 7

2 Fill in the gaps

Read the paragraph below and fill in the gaps with the words in the box. The first has been done for you.

> ravens   clever   o'clock   ~~unusual~~   sleep   cages
> job   eating   water   feathers

The Ravenmaster at the Tower of London has an (0) unusual, job: he looks after the (1)............... . He starts working at about five (2)............... in the morning because the birds wake up early. He lets the ravens out of their cages where they (3)............... at night. The ravens are always happy to see him.

Then he gives them food and (4)............... and cleans their cages. Ravens like (5)............... red meat, boiled eggs and biscuits. They live about twenty-five years.

Every three weeks the Ravenmaster and another Yeoman cut a few (6)............... off the right wings of the ravens. In this way they can fly close to the ground but they can't fly away. The Ravenmaster says the birds are very (7)............... and listen to him. When it's time to go to sleep he calls them and they go to their (8)............... for the night.

The Ravenmaster says, 'I'm the king raven because I'm part of their family. I've got a great (9)............... because I'm the only Ravenmaster Yeoman in the world!'

If you climb to the top of the dome, you will get a wonderful view of London.

When we are thinking about a possible situation in the future we use:

if + present verb, future verb

If he **knows** French and Spanish, he'**ll get** the job.

If I **have** time, I'**ll** visit the British Museum.

This kind of sentence is often called 'the first conditional'.

7 ACTIVITIES

3 First conditional
Complete the first conditional sentences with the verbs from the box.

> be   have   find   write   catch   see   go

1 If we don't hurry, we .... late for the theatre.
2 If I .... a London guide book, I'll buy it for you.
3 If it doesn't rain, they .... to Soho for lunch.
4 If you go to Piccadilly Circus, you .... the parade.
5 If Susan .... from London, he'll give you her letter.
6 If Jack gets up early, we .... the early morning train to London.
7 If the students .... time, they'll join us at the Tower.

KET 4 Notices
Which notice (A-H) says this (1-5)? There is an example at the beginning (0).

0 **B** You can rent a flat here.
1 ☐ You can visit this place on weekends.
2 ☐ If you hurt yourself, go to this place.
3 ☐ You need personal identification if you want to enter here.
4 ☐ They opened in the 18th century.
5 ☐ You can't buy a train ticket before 6 am.

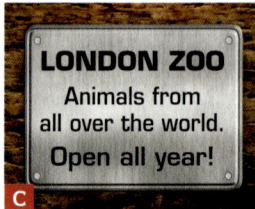

ACTIVITIES 7

  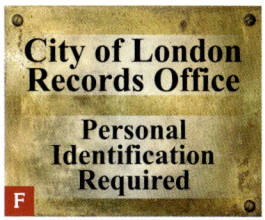

INTERNET PROJECT

Let's visit the London Eye!

The London Eye is also known as the Millennium Wheel, and it is one of the world's biggest wheels that you can ride and an exciting tourist attraction. You can get a wonderful view of London from the Eye. It was inaugurated on 31 December 1999 just before the third millennium. Divide the class into three groups and each one can do research and present a brief report to the class on: History, Making of the London Eye and Interesting Facts.

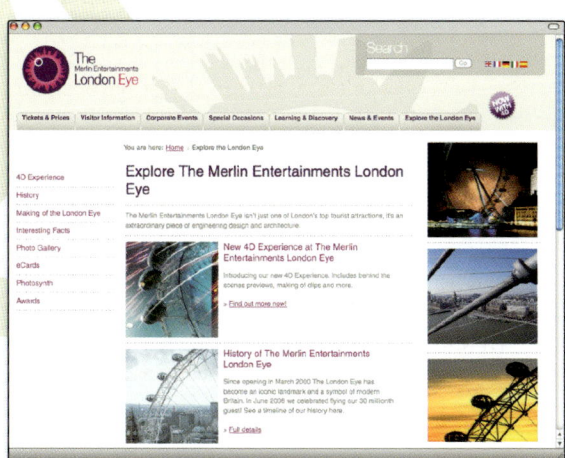

AFTER READING

1 Comprehension check

Are these sentences 'Right' (A) or 'Wrong' (B)? If there is not enough information to answer 'Right' (A) or 'Wrong' (B), choose 'Doesn't say' (C). There is an example at the beginning (0).

		A	B	C
0	Londinium was part of the Roman province called Britannia.	✓	☐	☐
1	In the Middle Ages the City was the centre of monarchy and religion.	☐	☐	☐
2	The theatre became a popular form of entertainment in Elizabethan London.	☐	☐	☐
3	It took five years for Shakespeare and the Lord Chamberlain's Men to build the Globe Theatre in Southwark.	☐	☐	☐
4	Samuel Pepys wrote about the plague and the Great Fire of London in the London newspaper.	☐	☐	☐
5	Inigo Jones and Christopher Wren were two great British architects who changed London's appearance.	☐	☐	☐
6	Dickens's London was a centre of industry and trade and the world's largest city.	☐	☐	☐
7	The Blitz took place between the two World Wars.	☐	☐	☐
8	One hundred twenty famous writers are buried in Poets' Corner of Westminster Abbey.	☐	☐	☐
9	The British Prime Minister's residence is in Whitehall.	☐	☐	☐
10	London's best department stores are open every day of the year.	☐	☐	☐
11	Charing Cross Road has many fine bookshops.	☐	☐	☐
12	The Tower of London is a performing arts centre in the City with a theatre and an art gallery.	☐	☐	☐

AFTER READING

2 Who was it?

Match the description (1-12) with the name (A-L). You can use a name more than once.

1. ☐ They invaded Britain in 43 CE.
2. ☐ He was a Saxon king.
3. ☐ He was the first Norman king.
4. ☐ He was a great Victorian writer.
5. ☐ He performed in the plays he wrote.
6. ☐ She was a great patron of the arts.
7. ☐ He was king of Scotland and England.
8. ☐ He brought Renaissance architecture to Britain.
9. ☐ He built a big sewer system in Victorian London.
10. ☐ She was the first monarch to live in Buckingham Palace.
11. ☐ He introduced the printing press to England.
12. ☐ He looks after the birds at the Tower of London.

A James I
B Roman Army
C William Shakespeare
D William the Conqueror
E Sir Joseph Bazalgette
F Edward the Confessor
G William Caxton
H Inigo Jones
I Elizabeth I
J Queen Victoria
K Ravenmaster
L Charles Dickens

3 A trip to London

Work with a partner and plan your trip to London. Say how you plan to get there, where you want to stay, how long you want to stay and what you want to visit and why. Present your plan to the class and… enjoy your trip!

This reader uses the **EXPANSIVE READING** approach, where the text becomes a springboard to improve language skills and to explore historical background, cultural connections and other topics suggested by the text.

The new structures introduced in this step of our **READING & TRAINING** series are listed below. Naturally, structures from lower steps are included too. For a complete list of structures used over all the six steps, see *The Black Cat Guide to Graded Readers*, which is also downloadable at no cost from our website, blackcat-cideb.com.

The vocabulary used at each step is carefully checked against vocabulary lists used for internationally recognised examinations.

Step **One A2**

All the structures used in the previous levels, plus the following:

Verb tenses
Present Simple
Present Continuous
Past Simple
Past Continuous
Future reference: Present Continuous;
 going to; *will*; Present Simple
Present Perfect Simple: indefinite past
 with *ever, never* (for experience)

Verb forms and patterns
Regular and common irregular verbs
Affirmative, negative, interrogative
Imperative: 2nd person; *let's*
Passive forms: Present Simple; Past
Simple
Short answers
Infinitives after verbs and adjectives
Gerunds (verb + *-ing*) after prepositions
 and common verbs
Gerunds (verb + *-ing*) as subjects
 and objects

Modal verbs
Can: ability; requests; permission
Could: ability; requests
Will: future reference; offers; promises;
 predictions
Would ... like: offers, requests
Shall: suggestions; offers
Should (present and future reference):
 advice

May (present and future reference):
 possibility
Must: personal obligation
Mustn't: prohibition
Have (got) to: external obligation
Need: necessity

Types of clause
Co-ordination: *but; and; or; and then*
Subordination (in the Present Simple or
 Present Continuous) after verbs such as:
 *to be sure; to know; to think; to believe;
 to hope; to say; to tell*
Subordination after: *because, when, if*
 (zero and 1st conditionals)
Defining relative clauses with: *who,
which,
that*, zero pronoun, *where*

Other
Zero, definite and indefinite articles
Possessive *'s* and *s'*
Countable and uncountable nouns
*Some, any; much, many, a lot; (a) little,
(a) few; all, every*; etc.
Order of adjectives
Comparative and superlative of
adjectives
 (regular and irregular)
Formation and comparative/superlative
 of adverbs (regular and irregular)